GOD'S
WORD

P.J. GREEN

ISBN 978-1-7328710-1-4 (paperback)
Copyright © 2020 by P.J. Green

All rights reserved. No part of this publication may be reproduced, distributed, or transmitted in any form or by any means, including photocopying, recording, or other electronic or mechanical methods without the prior written permission of the publisher. For permission requests, solicit the publisher via the address below.

Green's Corner

Waxahachie, TX
www.christianfaithpublishing.com

Printed in the United States of America

DEDICATION

To my parents:

Their love: "bears all things, believes all things, hopes all things, endures all things."
Their love "never fails."
1 Corinthians 13:1

Their treasure was not monetary--it was my mother's eyes that saw God's presence wherever she was. My dad who always believed in me--and always lived for his family.

Phillip – my brother – who whatever he does in life puts his heart and soul into it.

Tommy – my younger brother – he has met many challenges in life – and has successfully walked the road of life and reached out for God's Loving Hands.

My son – Christopher Brian Green – who everyday I am amazed at the person you are and the person you are becoming.

My daughter in law who of all the women in the world I would have chosen you to be Brian's wife.

My husband – You are my dreams come true. Today, Tomorrow & Always.

To My Friend – Sherron Kosco Foster. I miss you today more than yesterday.

GOD IS THE GREAT POTTER

YOU ARE HIS VESSEL

PJ Green's purpose in writing this book is to allow the reader to see how although mountains are difficult to overcome at times—if you slow down long enough and listen God will:

Direct your path—Proverbs 3:6

God is the great potter. He is molding you into a vessel that will be:

Prepared for every good work—2 Tim 2:21

Mountains along one's way are gifts from God to make you into the vessel you were meant to be. They are extremely difficult at times and you might question "why me"—but years down the road you will realize those mountains made you the person you are today.

No matter where you are in life, you serve a purpose. You will become the vessel that will truly light up people's lives. Until you draw you last breath—look around you—be the vessel God designed you to be.

"You are my hiding place: You shall preserve me from trouble."

Ps 32:7

God understands that every once in a while our bodies and souls need a little time away in order to replenish ourselves.

In fact it is during those times when our relationship with God grows even stronger.

"Lift up your eyes on high And see who has created these things."

Is 40:26

Nature adds serenity to one's life. One can accumulate worldly goods and still have an emptiness within their souls.

Where it is true that God forgives if asked—sometimes I feel I have blown it so badly in life—I ask,

"How could he forgive?"

I guess when I consider how I have fallen and he has forgiven me, it makes it easier for me to forgive others. For in all reality, we are all flawed individuals.

I am the vine,
you are the branches
John 15:5

Take time to look at trees. Their branches generally aim upward. You will also notice that each branch needs the other branch. It is just like our need for God, family, friends, etc. God is at the base of the tree holding up the branches.

"Whoever rejects you rejects me."

Lk 10:16

God asks very little from us. He wants us to "treat each other as we would want others to treat ourselves." It is not possible to reject someone in life and not reject God.

Look at the swan gracefully gliding across the river. They have no concerns. They are so deeply in love with nature and the very gift of the very air that they breathe.

"For God hath not given us the spirit of fear; but of power, and of love, and of a sound mind"

2 Tm 1:7

Fear is from the devil. It takes over the whole body and soul, and the individual leads a life of darkness. It is during this time that the devil is pulling you with all his might. Every time you slow down and really start questioning the fear that has overtaken your life, the devil pulls you down and uses all its energy to keep you down.

"They shall still bring forth fruit in old age."
Ps 92:14

Being old is just a frame of mind. When one stops living because they are old, what they are doing is cheating the world of their knowledge and experience that comes from living many years. Not only must you touch other people's lives, but you must allow others to touch your life. Always remember until you take your last breath, you still serve a purpose. It may be the person you meet tomorrow. It may be the homeless person on the street that could use a friendly hello. Whatever it is, look around; it is there.

"He makes my feet like the feet of a dear; he enables me to stand on the heights."

Ps 18:33

One must always seek new adventures in life. In seeking new adventures, many times fear (which comes from the devil) overcomes you and limits everything that you do. It is important that at this time, you lean on your faith and let the light of God's love in.

"There is a time for everything, and a season for every activity under the heavens."

Eccl 3:1

Do not be fearful of different seasons in one's life. Some will be happy and some will devastate you. Realize that God is there with you in the happiest of times and the saddest of times.

"My grace is sufficient for you, for My strength is made perfect in weakness. Therefore, most gladly "I will rather boast in my infirmities, that the power of Christ may rest upon me."

2 Cor. 12:9

Everyone has different strengths and weaknesses. Do not be fearful when your weakness is being challenged for the "power of Christ" will rest upon you. "It is God who arms me with strength and keeps my way secure."

Psalm 18:32

---ornament---

"I am bankrupt without love."

1 Cor 13:3

Imagine what the world or for that matter, your life would be like if there was no love in the world.

---ornament---

"As a face is reflected in water, so the heart reflects the real person."

Prv 27:19

A person who has darkened his soul and his heart is easily spotted. Negativity is all this person has to offer. It surrounds his very being.

"Therefore I take pleasure in informalities in reproaches, in needs, in persecutions, in distresses, for Christ's sake. For when I am weak, then I am strong."
2 Cor 12:10

My heart hurts
My body aches

I must be strong
For those around me

For being so strong
I feel so weak

"Therefore, humble yourselves under the mighty hand of God, that he may exalt you in due time, casting all your care upon him for he cares for you."

1 Peter 5:6-7

So often we feel that we are all by ourselves – feeling so much darkness surrounding us. It is during times when the weight of so many problems seems to consume our very existence. This is the time when we must humble ourselves – and ask for God to help us. We must not only talk to him but it is most important that you listen to what he is saying. It is also important that you allow him to show you the way – and realize that his way may not be your way.

"Set your mind on things above—not on things on the earth."

Col 3:2

Dear Father, you guided me when I was lost. I felt I had nothing to offer. It was at one of my darkest hours and yet you still loved me.

I confess that I still need your help. A part of my life needs your touch. Satan is battling for my soul. Please I beg don't let him win. Please defeat him.

I will give you the glory.

"Stop quarreling with God."

Job 22:21.

A cross *which* we carry *is* a work of God in our lives. We must embrace it and go forward with it. We must discover how God wants us to best use our experiences in life to serve him.

When you lose someone dear to you—know this—it is a gift he has given you. There are others he could have given it to, but he entrusted you with this gift. For it is not everyone who has the heart and soul and love as you do, who will so freely share it with all those left behind.

"For God has not given us a spirit of fear."
2 Tim 1:7

The building blocks of life are a sum of all the experiences of one's life. What is important is the growth behind each of the blocks. Did one grow from the good and bad experiences of life, or did one become bitter and only see darkness and not the wonders of the world all around them?

"God is not the author of confusion but of peace."
1 Cor 14:33

Today it snowed. The snow makes me think of my life right now.

My heart, soul, and body are nothing like the snow—they are so heavy.

But then again I am like the snow—so light. Anything blows me away. Anything blows me off the beaten path.

The snow is perfect in its beauty. The snow shares its beauty with all around. The snow is God's love made perfect.

"You will call, and the Lord will answer; you will cry for help, and he will say "Here I am".

Is 58:9

God sees us through our good times and our bad times.
There are times when we turn our back to him. Times when we are running away from His love as fast as we can.
So often we look for him, and we say we can't find him.
He has always been there.

"Consider it all joy when you encounter various trials."

James 1:2

I have always found it difficult to forgive myself. It has always been hard for me to accept the fact that God has already forgiven me.

I must realize that Christ was not perfect. One of the reasons he came to Earth was so that he could take the human form. He showed anger several times and he showed where he wanted to take the easy way out and not be crucified. However, he followed His father's will.

My challenge in life is to forgive myself and for once accept the fact that I have fallen and will fall again but realize that he will be there to forgive me.

"I can do everything through him."

Phil 4:13

My past is nonexistent for God.
It is what I do with today that is important to him.

"If we confess our sins, he is faithful and just and will forgive us."

1 John 1:9

God wants you to get over being angry with yourself. As long as you don't forgive yourself and are still angry at yourself, you can't be used to your fullest potential.

"I am with you always."

Matt 28:20

Sometimes people try to think too much when it comes to God.

That is where your faith comes in. It is not for you to figure out mysteries that have no human answers.

God sends the Holy Spirit to reside in your heart and soul.

He asks you only to use your heart and not your head to accept what you know is true. If one has no faith, there is an emptiness within the person that can't be satisfied. It is not a hunger for food; it is a yearning for God's love and acceptance.

"He will not let you be tempted beyond what you can bear."

1 Cor 10:13

I have been blown away so often in my life. My faith has been bent with troubles (large and small) that have come my way. There is a voice that calls my name, but I know better. There is a voice that wants only good for me and tells me to slow down and not to worry, but I know better.

I consider all the years, what have I accomplished? I'm just a body that is twice its age and a soul as dark as night.

I resolve to live in the light and allow the light to lead the way.

"For God did not give us a spirit of timidity."
2 Tim 1:7

I am thankful for the road I have traveled in life.
I don't exclude any roads.
For all the roads I have traveled were meant to be traveled by me. They form who I am today.
Some took years to travel—me dragging my feet all the way.
Some I grew from. Some destroyed my inner soul for a while.
On some roads, darkness encircled me.
But as the darkness lifts, there is always a beautiful light to lead the way.

"Let us throw off everything that hinders."

Heb 12:1

There are times when I feel like I am pulling a wagon that has one hundred pounds of meat in it.

In Matthew 11:28–30, the word yoke is mentioned. Yokes are wooden frames on the shoulders of oxen to help them pull a heavy load. Being yoked to God is the answer to my worries and stresses in life.

I can carry the load by myself, but it will take its toll on me and those around me. I need to be still and give him the load. I allow him to teach me that I do not control my life—he does—and he will be there walking beside me all the way.

"Trust in the Lord with all thine heart; and lean not unto thine own understanding."

Prov. 3:5

So often I have had sleepless nights, lying and worrying about what tomorrow may bring.

Instead of worrying about the unknown, I will give God a beautiful package with blue and green paper. I am giving it to God with a red bow on top. The red bow is my love for him and God's love for me.

The package will be my life—however long I may live—my total self. I understand that there will be times when I will fail, but it is my desire and hope that it is at those times I ask for forgiveness and forgive myself.

"Except you be converted, and become as little children, you shall not enter into the kingdom of heaven."
Mat 18:3

The rain is God's love for everyone. He rains on all with his love and understanding. He showers his love on everyone no matter what you have done in your life.

With the morning comes new life. It is God giving you the opporunity to use it to honor him.

God wants to use you wherever your place in life is—wherever you may find yourself.

"In all your ways acknowledge him, and he shall direct they paths."

Prov 3:6

I walk the twisted path of life
Only to be blown over by a
Gust of wind
My footing loses all balance
And I stumble along the path
Another path I seek out
The wind is continuously
Blowing in my face
There is a hill in front
I try and try to get to the top
I am on my knees crawling to
No avail
Another path I search out
It's straight no hill in sight
There is the beautiful valley
Where water is streaming from
The heavens.
I struggle to my feet

I can do this it is within my power
I can do this—I struggle and struggle
The water seems further and further away
The sun shines on it ever so brightly
In my frality, I fall to my knees
I have traveled the twisted and hilly
Paths of life
Stubbling all the way
Shouting down the voice inside of me
It is but a whisper
If I busy myself with other things, it
Will go away.
No, I can still hear it.
It is like an emptiness down deep inside
I have all the world has to offer
But there is still emptiness
Run—I must continue to run
That way I don't hear it
What is it saying
I'm not ready today—

Maybe tomorrow will be a
Better day.
I will slow down then and
Listen
But to my avail to my dismay
Tomorrow never comes.

"You will keep him in perfect peace—Whose mind is stayed on You."

Isiah 26:3

One's life encompasses many, many moments. Their life is like a jigsaw puzzle with 1,000 pieces, some happy, some sad, some fearful, some joyful, some good moments, and some bad.

One's journey through life is a long bumpy one, full of speed bumps and detours.

Often the road becomes somewhat like a merry-go-round. (as it was for Moses). It is those times when one gets stuck and keeps circling around a hole as deep as one can see. It is that hole that fends off any happiness that may come its way, for it is not a hole; it is hell. It is dark and empty and a very lonely place. Until the merry-go-round stops, life is based on that person's hell.

One must make peace with their own hell and acknowledge that something happened in their life which has left a mark on their very soul, for once the merry-go-roound stops, the bumps and detours in life will be easily overcome.

"Lay up for yourselves treasure in heaven."

Matt 6:20

I am in awe of you my Father in heaven. You still love me and care about me after all that I have done and after all I have not done that I should have done.

I never want to complain to You. You have given me so much. It is hard for me to tell You my worries, my concerns, my hurts, etc.

For as long as I don't tell him my worries and concerns I am in control.

---⋄○⋞∞⋟○⋄---

"We all like sheep, have gone astray."

Is 53:6

I lay down to go to sleep and what I envisioned was a lost sheep. He was lost—not knowing where he was going—running frantically around in circles, tired, frustrated but running at the speed of light to nowhere.

I envisioned a sheep huddled in a corner somewhere, ashamed and humiliated of all the mistakes made in the past, feeling so beaten down, so worthless, so unloveable.

I hear footsteps coming toward me—so firm and so sure, so strong, so deliberate. There is nowhere to hide or run to. He carries a staff. He is coming closer and closer. There is no sense in trying to hide.

He knows where I am. He knows who I am – and what I have done in my life. There is no judgment in his eyes. No judgment in his voice. He only says- I forgive you.

---⋄○⋞∞⋟○⋄---

"Fear Not"
             Luke 12:32

God has never forgotten me.

What has being in control done for me; it has aged me. It has made me so that I have stopped laughing. What would happen if I give up control of my life to you—the one whom I know, is in control.

If I give up control, there would be less sleepless nights. I would start seeing the beauty around me. There would not be a tense bone in my body. I would have problems, but I would ask you to continue to be in control.

Our Son

Our son is a man among men.
What might you ask makes him a man among men
He hides not his love for family, friends and the stranger on the street.
Is he a doctor or lawyer you might ask
Does he live in a castle
No, the gold in his life he finds is not in things
No, it is in people
The beauty around him
His family and close friends
His parents would both tell you it's the way he lives his life, his morals, especially that he is a man of principle
This is our son
You will recognize him if you ever meet him
For he will stand head and shoulder above all.

About the Author

P. J. Green has spent the last twenty-five years journaling her friends, family, and her own valleys and mountains. Through such a process, she has been able to learn from those mountains and not continuously relive the mistakes of the past.

Her faith has been strengthened, and she no longer wonders why things happened – but instead looks at those times as gifts from God. It is during these times that she has become the vessel God always intended her to be.

Pictures within this book were all taken by P. J. Green.

www.ingramcontent.com/pod-product-compliance
Lightning Source LLC
Chambersburg PA
CBHW031457040426
42444CB00007B/1137